THE POCKET LIBRARY OF GREAT ART

Plate 1. COURBET C. 1865. *Photo Pierre Petit.*
Lent by "Les Amis de Courbet"

GUSTAVE

COURBET

(1819-1877)

text by

ANDRÉ CHAMSON

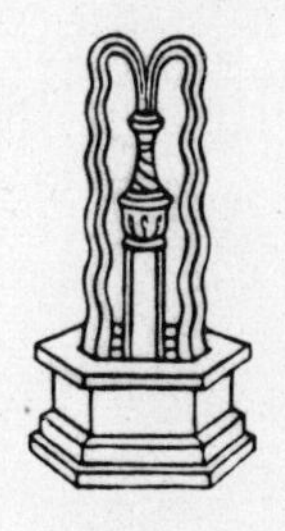

published by HARRY N. ABRAMS, INC., *New York*

On the cover

REFLECTION

(1864—66)

Museum of Douai, France

MILTON S. FOX, Editor.

Printed in The Netherlands, 1956, by Offset Smeets, Weert.

Plate 2. COURBET IN HIS CELL AT SAINTE-PÉLAGIE.
The Louvre, Drawing Room (portfolio R.F. 29235)

Courbet

"He is an eye!" Ingres exclaimed one day, speaking of Courbet, and this judgment, in which admiration and spite are mixed, is at the same time the most just and the most unjust evaluation possible about the Master of Ornans.

Marvelously rapid and precise, the eye of Courbet is in no way like the lens of a camera. It is not merely an eye. It is a way of seeing. It sees the world with an aspect possible only to our binocular vision; it is a vision which measures and compares all things; the gaze of a thinking being, a gaze full of tenderness or suffering.

It plunges to the depths of the self, into the marvelous universe called memory.

The eye of Courbet sees creature and universe by giving them this double dimension. This realist does not limit himself to painting the object before him. He *rediscovers* it. One might say that he made a pact with the universe, with its four constitutive elements, air and fire, water and earth. The reality that he sees always mingles with a reality already seen, a reality identified with the poetic universe he bears within him.

This universe is that of his childhood and youth, that of the gray skies of the Franche-Comté, the part of France he comes from; of the fires that flare between the pines on late afternoons in his town of Ornans, of the earth which clings to the giddy perpendiculars of the *Roche de Dix-Heures* (Ten O'Clock Rock), of the water which boils at the bottom of the *Puits Noir* (Black Pits). For him, all creation is organized around this bit of earth, this "country" in the oldest meaning of that word. It is from this domain that he sets out to conquer the world. To the gray skies of his Jura Mountains he adds the blue skies of Languedoc, and the tumultuous horizons of the Channel's shores; the water of the *Puits Noir* leads him towards the seas and their stormy waves. But he always remains a man of the region where he was born, the Master of Ornans, a rustic prince, a sort of feudal lord, as the notables of French provinces were so often during the last century.

A rustic prince at twenty, beautifully built, with an Assyrian face, he had the appearance, when mature, of a country lawyer or doctor, or of some hereditary owner of forests and pastures. He had the manner and the mind, the vulgarity and the nobility for such a station. He enjoyed the same diversions as the landowners:

Plate 3. Detail from AFTERNOON AT ORNANS. *1849. Palais des Beaux-Arts, Lille (Photo Bulloz)*

tracking deer in the snow to the depth of the woods where the streams begin, drinking the wines of the region, singing old songs. He always loved his mountains and valleys, and seems even to belong to some other land. For men of this breed, the countryside, the provinces, are their Fatherland. Nevertheless, no one is more French than he, or more profoundly linked to France, and therefore perhaps he is quite incomprehensible to one who does not understand France.

If he had not been a painter, Courbet would have been just a rustic of the Juras, like other men of these mountains. But he was a painter, and knew how to take from life what it gives to each of us as a fleeting, revocable offering, and to transform this into an eternal gift. Such is the miracle of an art brought to its perfection. In its consummation, every technique is itself a source of poetry, and the painter, in painting, gives birth to the poet. So what matters the theme or the subject? Everything serves as material for inspiration: the face of the artist, that of his father or his sisters, the stream that flows past his house and sinks in the gorges of the valley, the green fields of spring, the first snow of autumn on the uplands at the black edge of the forests. Anything is subject matter for one who has this sense of the real, this communion with life. One evening Courbet's mistress of twenty years leaned forward and on her cheek shone the last reflection of the sun. Nothing could be more commonplace, nothing more like what happens daily in the secret monotony of human lives. But that instant is now caught on canvas, in flaring lights and shadow, in the sumptuous textures which the artist handles as he pleases; and so thousands of men will know for centuries how much tenderness and happiness can be expressed in the last flicker of light on a woman's face.

Plate 4. Detail from BURIAL AT ORNANS. *1850.*
The Louvre

Plate 5. Detail from THE STUDIO *(center section). 1855. The Louvre*

Plate 6. Detail from THE STUDIO *(right-hand section, with Baudelaire reading). 1855. The Louvre*

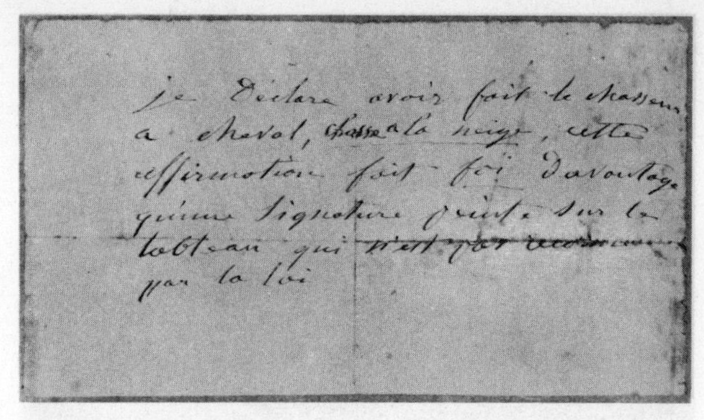

je Déclare avoir fait la chasse
a cheval, chasse a la neige, cette
affirmation fait foi davantage
qu'une signature peinte sur la
tableau qui ~~n'est pas reconnue~~
par la loi

Plate 7. Facsimile of Courbet's handwritting. Declaration of having hunted on horseback for his *Hunting in the Snow*

Every great creator carries within him the power to produce new things. It is through painting that Courbet enlarged his world. He added new skies to the ones he discovered during his childhood, new faces to those he saw during his youth. The day came when, after having restricted himself, with chaste discretion, to modeling the faces of his sisters, he could put into his works the beautiful naked bodies and faces of women, heavy with sensuality and fleshly grace. In the fullness of his powers, crushing his colors under the blade of his knife to arrange them in an architecture of lights, he understood that the fullness of beauty lies perhaps in the repose which follows the exaltation of life. It is doubtless at such moments that every being and every thing seems to have taken on something of an eternal character. It is at that point that the art of Courbet reaches perfection. No one knew better than he how to express the splendor of beautiful days — when shadows lie on the grass at the feet of trees; or the splendor of naked bodies between

Chef des dépêches

Citoyen Bernard

Eugène Grandperrin
négociant à Besançon
venu ici pour achats,
doit retourner dans
son pays.

Salut fraternel

Veuillez lui faire
avoir un passeport.

G. Courbet

Président des arts

Plate 8. Facsimile of a letter written by Gustave Courbet during the Commune and bearing his official title as President of the Arts Committee dream and awakening. Whether in his paintings *Siesta, The Sleepers,* and *Young Women on the Banks of the Seine,* he expressed plastically one of the solemn moments of life. Bodies lulled, their forces intact, the blossoming of flowers and trees, triumphant life in the secret heart of ordinary but complete things: a rose, an apple, a trout just drawn from the water — such are the themes he chose, themes only the very great knew how to treat, as he did. He is like Louis le Nain, and Chardin, in that his humblest still lifes express the world, but one has to go back to the "Pastoral Concerts" of Renaissance painting to find so perfect a resonance of cosmic rhythm on the human body.

What we call the "subject" — the mere identity — here loses all importance. But it was subject in another sense, however, that Courbet emphasized. For him this was a means of attaining liberty, but, once liberated, this realist invented a world, and became indistinguishable from the poets. Too often he has been judged in terms of his remarks and his writings, or even simply by the titles of his works. But who would think of judging Balzac or Stendhal by their drawings? An artist in words is never put to this test; he would seldom emerge bigger in stature. Language has other methods, and seeks other goals than the plastic arts. We admire in the books of certain painters their talent as writers, but this talent has nothing in common with their paintings, no, not even when it is the talent of a Delacroix. We must judge Courbet as a painter. The problem is not to try to understand him in terms of his theories, but on the contrary, to try to understand his theories after having entered fully the universe he created with his brush.

Every great creator escapes from his own definitions.

Plate 9. NO ENTRANCE! *by Alfred Le Petit.*
Lent by "Les Amis de Courbet"

Thus, while he thought his task was to found a Realist school, in actual fact the Master of Ornans opened the way for Impressionism. He discovered in his own way the luminous style in painting. Above all, he knew how to create a vital contact between creature and universal, a contact made of lightness and fullness, so that in his work poetry and reality mingle.

Plate 10. Prisoners of the Federation in the Grand Stables of Versailles, 1871. *The Louvre, Drawing Room (portfolio R.F. 29235)*

Then what matter to us the tumultuous events of his life — the battles for honors, the anecdotes and the legends, the calumnies, the persecutions and exile? There is no exile for him who bears in his heart a land he never forgets.

Courbet's hand might return to groping as in his youth; the lightning of his genius might now flash only through a thicker and thicker mist. But he had done his work. And when the hour came for him to drink his last glass of wine — "one for the road"; when the wave of our common fate engulfed forever this great artist on that last day of December, around the painter's deathbed some ripe fruits and a few faces of young girls reaffirmed the splendors of life.

Plate 11. PORTRAIT OF ZÉLIE COURBET. *c. 1855. Charcoal. Museum of Ornans*

Plate 12. WOMAN COMBING HER HAIR.
The Louvre, Drawing Room (portfolio R.F. 29234)

Plate 13. RUINS ON THE BANKS OF THE RHINE. *1856.*
The Louvre, Drawing Room

Plate 14. PRISONERS OF THE FEDERATION AT THE VERSAILLES ORANGERIE, *1871. The Louvre, Drawing Room (portfolio R.F. 29235)*

COLOR PLATES

PLATE 15

Painted c. 1842—44

ZÉLIE COURBET

Petit Palais, Paris

Oil, 15 x 13"

Zélie was the artist's second sister. She lived from 1828 to 1875. She appears again in *Young Women of the Village* and was the model for the *Sleeping Spinner.*

Her hair encircled with a dark red ribbon and decorated by a garland of leaves, which gives her a sort of rustic charm, Zélie's face is painted in the manner of Ingres, but without affection or conventionalization; the head is not unlike a bright flesh-colored fruit. In this portrait there is more sensuality than in the portrait of Juliette (see plate 18), and less chaste reserve. As beneath the exterior of the child one senses the girl, here one senses in the girl the blossoming of a young woman.

Plate 16. PORTRAIT OF THE ARTIST (COURBET WITH A BLACK D

(commentary follows color plate section)

Plate 17. WOUNDED MAN

(commentary follows color plate section)

PLATE 18

Painted 1844

JULIETTE COURBET

Petit Palais, Paris

Oil, 30¾ x 24⅜"

Courbet owes much to his sisters. They embellished the world of his childhood. All three were beautiful and charming in their youth, and their existence perhaps explains the feeling for elegance, grace, and fantasy which helped him to bring off his most poetic canvases. The sisters are responsible for the troop of young, chaste, and dreaming girls, who pass through his work, while his ephemeral love affairs inspired the beautiful, sensual nudes.

Juliette was the painter's favorite sister, the youngest and the most beautiful. She lived from 1832 to 1915, in devoted adoration of her brother, whose fame she promoted until the end of her life. It was she who, in 1909, bequeathed to the Petit Palais the group of works, including this picture, which make up one of the world's most beautiful Courbet collections.

Every detail in her portrait is classical. The armchair is treated as if by Philippe de Champaigne. The flowers recall those in the Herbal of Pierre Quthe by Clouet. The draperies and other fabrics are worthy of the portraitists of the eighteenth century. But this is a classicism which is very close to realism. To paint, in an Ingresque manner, this pure face of a budding young girl, is realist enough.

PLATE 19

Painted 1844

ELÉANOR RÉGIS COURBET

Collection Georges-René Laederich, Paris

Oil, 28¾ x 23½"

The father of the artist (1798—1882) was about 50 when his son made this portrait of him. It is of a man of landed property, half-bourgeois and half-peasant. Mac Buchon described him to Champfleury: "Realistic, a ceaseless talker, in love with nature, sober as an Arab, tall, long-limbed, immensely affectionate, always in his shirt sleeves, a seeker of ideas and agricultural improvements, the inventor of an improved cultivator, and devoted, despite his wife and daughters, to farming, from which he barely made a profit."

Courbet resembled his father physically; however, it was not from him that he inherited the well-marked brow which appears in all his portraits, nor the regrettable tendency to stoutness, further aggravated by dropsy during his last years. Stronger, more robust, and more of a peasant, the father outlived the son. He appears again in *After Dinner at Ornans,* in *The Burial,* and in a last portrait painted in 1874.

PLATE 20

Painted c. 1847

WOMAN COMBING HER HAIR

Collection A. Morhange, Esq., London

Oil, 21⅝ x 18⅛"

Just as he left the Franche-Comté of his youth, Courbet left Paris. He always disliked the beaten path, and this first visit abroad revealed to him the art of the Northern countries, then not in much favor. It was not to Italy that he turned, but to Holland and Belgium. The painting of Rembrandt won his complete admiration. He carefully studied *The Night Watch*. And no doubt he saw the work of Vermeer.

This lovely little picture, pervaded with a feeling of the intimacy and comfortable profusion of a Dutch room, reflects the admiration of the Master of Ornans for the masters of the Low Countries. Earthy and powerful, Courbet yet knew as well as any of them, the art of revealing the pearly quality of a neck, the delicacy of a hand, the whiteness of linen. He went even further in daring than those painters who evoked a face only by its reflection in a mirror; he here suggests the purity of a profile while hiding it behind a strand of heavy black hair.

PLATE 21

Painted c. 1851

THE MEUSE AT FREYR

Musée des Beaux-Arts, Lille

Oil, 27 x 32¼"

Courbet painted nature without regard for the picturesque. He was for painting the rocks and the river bends, taking them as they come. Doubtless he chose this spot because the rocks recalled those of Ornans, and the Meuse, the Loue. We see here how he broadened his world.

Charles Léger reports the remarks Courbet made in Switzerland, which show clearly what he demanded of nature. "You remind me of poor Baudelaire who, one evening in Normandy, took me at sunset to a rock, overlooking the sea. He brought me to a yawning gap framed by cut-out rocks: 'That's what I wanted to show you,' Baudelaire told me. 'That is the view. Is it bourgeois enough? What is a view? Does such a thing exist?'" To this painter's eye everything was subject matter for a painting.

The picture was acquired by the Museum of Lille in 1908.

PLATE 22

Painted 1854

THE MEETING
or BONJOUR, MONSIEUR COURBET

Fabre Museum, Montpellier

Oil, 50¾ x 58⅝"

Commissioned by Bruyas in 1854, this canvas represents the meeting of the painter and the great collector when the latter visited Courbet in Languedoc. It caused a scandal, not because of its style, but by its treatment of the figures. Courbet was not forgiven for his arrogant attitude, his thrust-out beard and stiff bearing, his Alpine outfit, and, especially, for the shadow, reserved for him alone, which doubled his own image. Banville expressed his disgust in the following verses:

> And the dark leafage scooped out like an arch,
> The grass plots, the bough bent by ripening fruit,
> Sang out: Good-day, Mr. Courbet, the master-painter,
> Mr. Courbet, Good-day. Bonjour, Mr. Courbet.

Today we are not much disturbed by the fact that Courbet drew his image with such self-satisfaction. Few painters have known how to render with such felicity the poetry of the open country burned by the hot June sun, the discolored greenery, and the dusty, flat roads; in the distance, a stage-coach may be seen. The whole artistry of Bazille is in this picture, and at one stroke the Master of Ornans has grasped the subtle spirit of the Mediterranean.

This picture was given to the Museum of Montpellier by Bruyas in 1868.

Plate 23. YOUNG WOMEN OF THE VILLAGE

(commentary follows color plate section)

PLATE 24

Painted c 1856—57

DOE LYING EXHAUSTED IN THE SNOW

Private collection

Oil, 35⅞ x 57⅞"

Courbet, a great hunter, like all the mountaineers of the Franche-Comté, loved to roam the woods with his friends. The hunt ended, he took delight in the long meals during which stories were told between songs. The drama of hunting never left him uninterested. There is great tenderness in the art with which he shows these animals, harassed and already mortally wounded, under a sky darker than the snow-covered earth. In other pictures he portrayed them free, confident, and happy. "This winter," he says in a letter to Cuénot, "I obtained some deer and built a shed for them. In the center a little doe sits, who receives like a hostess. It's just like in a salon. Beside her is her mate. It's most charming, and they're as prefect as diamonds."

G. Courbet.

PLATE 27

Painted 1866

THE SLEEPERS

Petit Palais, Paris

Oil, 53⅛ x 78¾"

A picture of Courbet's representing Venus and Psyche had been rejected by the Salon of 1864 as "improper." The painter's friends were up in arms. Proudhon wrote: "Courbet has undertaken to do for painting what moralists like Ezekiel and Juvenal did for poetry: to satirize the abominations of his time." And Castagnary: "This so-called preacher of immorality has always been an apostle of morality. He has spent his life in glorifying work, the family, honor, devotion. He would never be satisfied to exhibit nudes for their own sake. . . ."

Khalil Bey, one-time Turkish Ambassador to St. Petersburg then residing in Paris, came to see Courbet's studio and wanted to buy *Venus and Psyche,* the picture rejected by the Salon, but it was already sold. Courbet promised to make another and executed for him these sleeping girls, and two other pictures, which seem to have been lost. The *Sleepers* was purchased in Switzerland by the Petit Palais in 1953.

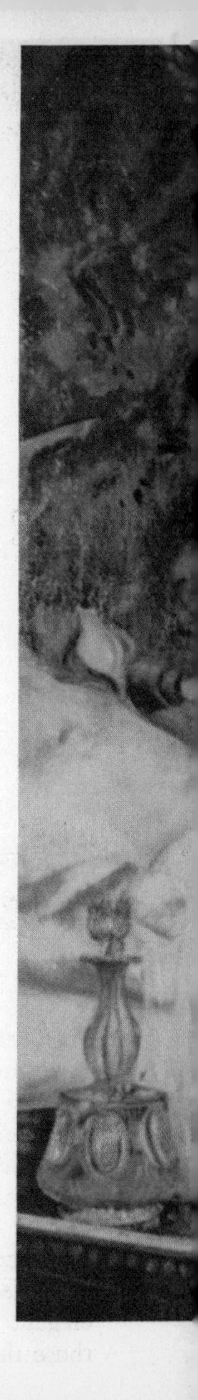

(commentary follows color plate section)

Plate 26. THE SLEEPING SPINNER

PLATE 25

Painted 1863

YOUNG GIRL ARRANGING FLOWERS

Toledo Museum of Art, Toledo, Ohio

Oil, 43¼ x 53⅛"

Invited to Rochemont, near Saintes, by Etienne Baudry, cousin of Théodore Duret, Courbet came in the spring of 1862 to this pretty place on the banks of the Charente. Here he spent his time painting, consuming good food and wine, telling stories, singing, and discussing literature and politics. Wishing to prolong his stay, but not wanting to inconvenience Baudry, he decided to stay at Saintes. Corot came to see him there and painted the same subjects with him. During this sojourn, which lasted until March, 1865, when he returned to Paris, Courbet painted many pictures of flowers. One of the most beautiful is this painting of a young woman at a trellis. One might have thought that Courbet was changing his style and orienting his art towards a new poetry, but this was not the case. The genius of the Master of Ornans expressed itself in oscillations, and not in the choice, or definite change, of manner. At the very time that he painted this picture, he also painted *Return from the Conference,* a burlesque of tipsy priests which scandalized the Salon of '63. The young woman at the trellis, is similar to the other young girls who appear in Courbet's work, and makes one think of the portrait of Juliette, of he girl with the seagulls, and of his little English girls.

PLATE 28

Painted 1864

SLEEPING REDHAIRED WOMAN

Collection Alfred Daber, Paris

Oil, 22½ x 27⅝″

This study of a sleeping woman, closely related to the canvas entitled *Venus and Psyche,* which was rejected by the Salon of 1864, marks a stage in Courbet's exploration of this theme which was to culminate, in 1866, with the masterpiece *The Sleepers.* The Master of Ornans had already painted female nudes, notably *The Bathers,* but these had been for the most part ample, heavily-fleshed figures. For the first time he now presented women with elegant forms who had nothing in common with those that had been called "draft horses."

G. Courbet.

Plate 29. YOUNG WOMEN ON THE BANKS OF THE SEINE

PLATE 31

Painted 1871

STILL LIFE WITH APPLES AND PEAR

Private collection, Paris

Oil, 10⅝ x 16⅛"

The recreations of a prisoner deprived of the good things of the earth, still lifes, executed for the most part from memory, are as truthful as if they had been painted from nature. (This one is signed and dated "G. Courbet, Ste-Pélagie, 71.") The eye of Courbet is a marvelous repository. Every reflection imprinted itself there for life, with its volumes, colors, and layers of light. These imagined objects longed for lovingly, symbols of Courbet's lost liberty, seem to take on a new beauty. A particular cluster of grapes, a certain red apple, become unusual objects, as if seen in a dream.

Gustave Courbet

PLATE 30

Painted 1863

PORTRAIT OF MADAME BOREAU

Private collection

Oil, 29½ x 23⅝″

Courbet met Mme. Boreau when he went to Saintonge. No doubt the painter was attracted to this beautiful face with its subdued tones, a delicate oval, with great, dark eyes like voluptuous circles, and to the romantic aspect of this somewhat sad figure in black. Mme. Boreau loved flowers, and it was doubtless because of her that Courbet painted flowers during this sojourn.

In this portrait Mme. Boreau is shown half-length, with transparent black lace at her throat. The blacks in the picture seem drenched with light. There is something secret in these melancholy eyes, a vague suggestion of the sadness of parting. Behind the slightly tilted face is a background of leaves and on the right one sees wooded hills, doubtless those overlooking the Charente.

(commentary follows color plate section)

G. Courbet

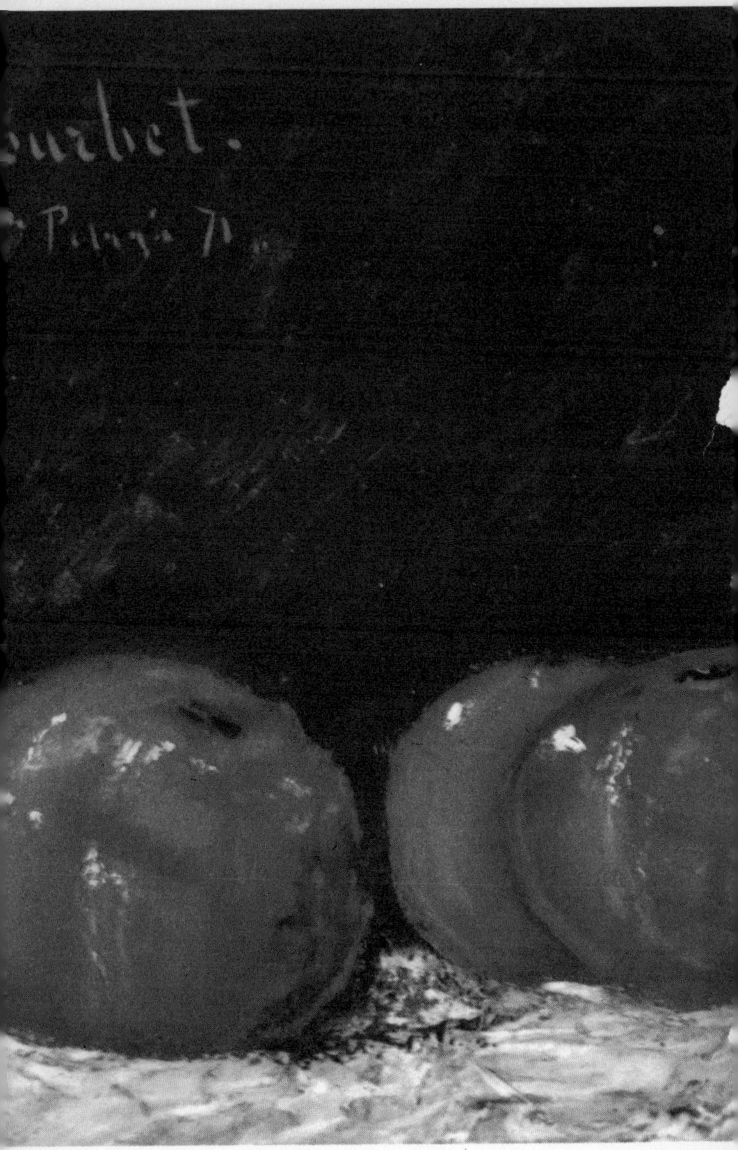

PLATE 32

Painted c. 1872

THE TROUT

Kunsthaus, Zurich

Oil, 20½ x 33½"

Despite the fact that this picture is dated 1871, and notwithstanding the statement in the artist's hand — *G. Courbet in vinculis faciebat* — this canvas was doubtless painted in 1872, at Ornans. Perhaps Courbet had made a drawing of this masterpiece when in Sainte-Pélagie; perhaps he simply wanted to show that he had painted works of this sort in prison. In any case, though he had declared that this work was "uncopiable," he made several replicas. One of them, a little larger than this one and with the trout's position reversed, is to be found in the collection of the painter Dunoyer de Segonzac. Rarely did Courbet express his feeling for nature with such force and simplicity. This trout, just drawn from the rushing waters, is still living.

Plate 33. THE GREAT OAK AT ORNANS

(commentary follows color plate section)

Plate 34. CLIFFS AT ETRETAT

(commentary follows color plate section)

PLATE 35

Painted 1871

COURBET AT SAINTE-PÉLAGIE

Museum of Ornans, France

Oil, 36¼ × 28½"

After the defeat of the Commune, Courbet was condemned to six months imprisonment for having participated in the demolition of the Vendôme Column: he was interned in Sainte-Pélagie. This prison, which was demolished in 1899, was situated between the Rue Monge and the Botanical Gardens. This self-portrait shows the painter seated at the window of his cell, dressed in prison garb, smoking his pipe. He has grown much thinner, the lines of his face are sunken, and his glance is sad. He was in such poor health that he was soon transferred to Dr. Duval's clinic in Neuilly.

To make imprisonment bearable, Courbet worked ceaselessly. "It is known that he made many attempts to set up a studio in his prison," says an art review of the epoch, cited by Léger. "While, to his great disgust, such authorization was not granted, he did obtain, some days afterwards, the right to have an easel, brushes, and colors brought him. . . ." This permitted Courbet to create several masterpieces, but he was not able to realize the desire he had at the time to paint the roofs of Paris, as he had painted the sea.

This picture was given, in 1903, to the Museum of Ornans by Juliette Courbet.

Painted c. 1842

PORTRAIT OF THE ARTIST (COURBET WITH A BLACK DOG)

Petit Palais, Paris

Oil, 18⅛ x 21⅝"

From 1840 on, Gustave Courbet lived in Paris. He was a handsome young man, tall and slender, with large and gentle eyes. Sylvestre claimed to see something Assyrian in his face, with its deep planes and very marked brow. This Oriental effect was emphasized when Courbet wore a beard. In this portrait he is still beardless, and with long, black hair. He is here the rustic prince who has just arrived in the capital. A little black spaniel, a recent gift to the artist, sits beside him. "This dog," said the painter, "is admired by everyone. He is more fussed over than I am. . . ."

Seated against the light, at the foot of a rock, with his head thrown back, Courbet portrayed himself in a romantic attitude. But he was twenty-three years old then and romanticism was flourishing. This melancholy Werther-like hero is, nevertheless, already the painter of Ornans. The rocks behind him are at the entrance of the Grotto of Plaisir-Fontaine, in the valley of Bonnevaux. They are like the high rocks of the Jura Mountains, which we find again and again in his canvases. Behind him is the cloudy sky of Franche-Comté, which spreads out over a wide, bright, and beautiful valley.

This picture was shown at the Salon of 1844.

Painted 1844

WOUNDED MAN

The Louvre, Paris

Oil, 31⅞ x 38⅛"

This is one of the most romantic of Courbet's long series of self-portraits. In this half-length portrait, the artist is leaning against a tree, next to the sword which wounded him. His eyes half-closed, his hair long, more Assyrian than ever now that his beard is full, he looks a legendary knight struck down while seeking the Grail, but his sufferings seem to dissipate themselves in the serenity of nature.

"During my life I made many self-portraits corresponding to changes in my spiritual make-up," Courbet told Bruyas in 1854. "In a word, they are my autobiography (*J'ai écrit ma vie*). The third [portrait] was of a man gasping out his life.... There is one that I've yet to make. It will be of the man certain of his principles, the free man...."

The portrait referred to was never painted by Courbet, unless we can recognize it, stripped of all romanticism and all anecdote, in the Courbet with the striped collar at the Museum of Montpellier, or in the Courbet of *The Studio.*

Rejected by the Salons of 1844, 1846, and 1847, *Wounded Man* was acquired by the State in the sale of 1881.

Painted 1851

YOUNG WOMEN OF THE VILLAGE

City Art Gallery, Leeds

Oil, 21⅝ x 26"

The *Young Women of the Village* are the artist's three sisters. Zoé, the future Mme. Reverdy, wears a big hat, Juliette carries a parasol, and Zélie, a basket on her arm, is giving alms to a shepherdess. This little group, with a dog, a bull, and a heifer, has stopped in a green glen surrounded by rocks, among which we see Ten O'Clock Rock. Carefully dressed in long skirts, Courbet's sisters seem better dressed for visiting than for walking in the fields. At that time it was thought proper to dress in this way for a walk in the country. The countryside, green and fresh, suggests the valley of the Loue in spring. The picture brought the painter a few compliments, but the figures in it were ferociously criticized. The subject, clearly conforming to the traditions of the provinces, doubtless upset the Parisian public. Edmond About declared that it was "an excellent landscape spoiled by the presence of some anomalous figures."

This canvas, in the Museum of Leeds, is a study for the big picture now in the Metropolitan Museum of New York, which was shown at the Salon of 1852 and acquired before the opening by the Comte de Morny.

Painted 1853

THE SLEEPING SPINNER

Fabre Museum, Montpellier

Oil, 35⅞ x 45¼"

This sleeping spinner is the second sister of the artist, the tender and modest Zélie. She no longer resembles the portrait her brother made of her as a young girl (plate 15), with her hair covered with leaves. Her features are coarser, her figure heavier, only her hands remain delicate. When she died in 1875, Gustave wrote Juliette: "I have cried out every tear in my body, I have wept for my poor Zélie, who had no other pleasure in life than to serve others and to please them."

The Sleeping Spinner is almost a representation of the girl's fate. Zélie was always serving the family, along with her mother, and like her, strove to make the others happy. Zélie became an old maid, while Zoé, married to the unhappy Reverdy, became her brother's enemy.

The picture was a success at the Salon of 1853. The conventional and tranquil character of the subject reassured the critics who had been scandalized by *The Bathers*. "There is also a *Sleeping Spinner*," said Delacroix, "presenting the same qualities of bold painting and representation. The spinning wheel, the distaff — admirable; the dress, the armchair — heavy and lacking grace. . . ." The spinning wheel was sold November 21, 1847 at a Drouot sale, in Paris. Acquired by Bruyas in 1853, the picture was given by him to the Museum of Montpellier in 1868.

Painted c. 1856

YOUNG WOMEN ON THE BANKS OF THE SEINE

Petit Palais, Paris

Oil, 68⅛ x 80¾"

"Impossible to stick to one woman if one wants to know about women," wrote Courbet. All were good to paint, and those most generous with their bodies made marvelous models. When he painted prostitutes, did he want to stigmatize evil, as he liked to claim? In the *Young Women on the Banks of the Seine* did he wish as Castagnary wrote, "to thunder against impudence and lewd laziness"?

If Courbet's intention had been to moralize, he evidently lost it in the fire of executing his picture, for he gave these sinners all the attractions of feminine ornament: silk and transparent net and muslin, shawls from the Indies, embroidered gloves, laces, and bracelets. They rest on a grass carpet, sprinkled with flowers, reminiscent of *Unicorn* tapestries. The faces may be thickened and puffy with sleep, but they do not convey the impression that sin is repugnant, as Courbet liked to claim. And what enchantment surrounds them! The tree throws a magnificent shadow. The Seine reflects a beautiful sky with its clouds. The boat awaits the pleasure of the young girls. Whether morality is or is not important in it, this picture is perhaps the masterwork of Courbet, one of those before which he could say with his naive pride: "What a piece! Is it painted? It's perfect!"

COMMENTARY FOR PLATE 33

Painted 1864

THE GREAT OAK AT ORNANS

Pennsylvania Academy of Fine Arts, Philadelphia

Oil, 35 x 43¼″

This sturdy oak of Ornans rivals the massive tree paintings of Poussin and Lorrain, the autumnal verdure of Watteau, the chestnut trees of Théodore Rousseau, the stripped woods of Millet, and Corot's elms of the Ile de France. One could make a sylvan geography from the works of these great painters, and in this map of the trees of France, Ornans, thanks to Courbet, would have a privileged place.

In his youth, Courbet had already painted this Ornans oak on whose trunk he had written his name beside that of one of his early loves: "Lise and Gustave." He was to repaint it once more, in a picture shown in 1867. There was a kind of secret alliance, a hidden relationship, a symbolic correspondence, between the Master of Ornans and this immense tree rooted in the soil of the Franche-Comté.

Painted 1869

CLIFFS AT ETRETAT

The Louvre, Paris

Oil, 51⅛ x 63¾"

During his stay in Languedoc, Courbet had come to understand the Mediterranean wonderfully. The sea attracted, but troubled, this mountaineer. He expresses this sentiment in a strange letter to Victor Hugo: "I admit it, I love dry land and the orchestra of numberless herds in our mountains. The sea, the sea with all its charms, saddens me! In its joy it affects me like a laughing tiger; in its sadness it reminds me of crocodile tears; and in its growling it has the fury of a caged monster who cannot gulp me down."

Nevertheless, Courbet was a great painter of the sea. In 1869, staying at Etretat with Diaz and the latter's son, he executed several admirable seascapes. More than ever he opened the way for Impressionism. Monet and Van Gogh were inspired by his vast marine skies, his rocks, and his boats.

This picture appeared in the Salon of 1870 and was acquired by the Louvre at the Charles André sale of 1914.

Troisième année. — N° 66. 9 Juin 1867

F. POLO

D. LEVY

LA LUNE

COURBET, GILL

Plate 36. CARICATURE, BY GILL. *1867.*
Lent by "Les Amis de Courbet"

BIOGRAPHICAL NOTES

1819	June 10. Birth of Jean Désiré Gustave Courbet at Ornans, in the Doubs region. His father, Eléonor Régis Courbet, owned a large estate at Flagey and vineyards at Ornans. His mother, Sylvie Oudot, came from Ornans.
1831	Courbet enters the small Ornans seminary. He is not a good student. In 1837 goes to the college of Besançon.
1840	November. Courbet comes to Paris. Devotes himself to painting.
1844	Gets first showing at the Salon with his *Courbet with a Black Dog.* Works furiously, as he did all his life.
1847—48	Spends eight days in Holland during the summer. Meets Baudelaire and many important writers and journalists.
1849	Seven canvases accepted at the Salon.
1849—50	Paints *Burial at Ornans.*
1855	After the Salon's rejection of *The Studio* and *Burial* he organizes a private exhibition on the Avenue Montaigne, where he shows 40 paintings and 4 drawings. His preface to the catalogue is a manifesto in favor of Realism. Goes to Belgium.
1857	Paints *Young Women on the Banks of the Seine.* Brussels Exhibition.
1858—59	Trip to Frankfort. Trip to Havre and to Honfleur with Boudin.
1862	Courbet opens a studio on the Rue Notre Dame de Champs. Sojourn at Saintonge.

1865	Finishes *Proudhon and his Children* after Proudhon's death. At Trouville meets Whistler and Jo, the Irish girl, who becomes his model.
1867	New exhibition at Rond-point de l'Alma.
1869	Trip to Etretat.
1870	Courbet refuses the Legion of Honor. July 14, war; September 14, the Republic. Courbet named President of a Committee for the preservation of works of art.
1871	April 12. The Commune decides to demolish the Vendôme Column. April 16. Courbet named Commune councillor and assigned to the Beaux Arts. May 11. Courbet resigns. May 16. Vendôme Columns demolished. Sept. 2. Courbet tried and condemned to six months imprisonment at Sainte-Pélagie.
1872	Undergoes surgery at Dr. Duval's clinic. May 26. Returns to Ornans.
1873	May 30. The Assembly decides to make him pay for the reconstruction of the Vendôme Column. July 23. Finds refuge in Switzerland at the Tour de Peilz of Bon Port.
1875	Death of Zélie. Exhibition at Bon Port.
1877	May 4. Ordered to pay 323,000 francs for the rebuilding of the Vendôme Column. Nov. 26. Government sale of the contents of Courbet's Rue Hautefeuille studio in Paris. Dec. 31. Courbet's death.
1919	His body is brought to the Ornans Cemetery.

SOME OPINIONS ABOUT COURBET

1849. "This young man, he is an eye. . . ." Ingres

1850. About *Burial at Ornans:* "We do not consider this picture a serious work." Clément de Ris Ris

"In the history of modern art, the *Burial* is Realism's columns of Hercules." Paul Mantz

1853. About *The Bathers*: "But now that M. Courbet has shown us his backside, what the devil will he come up with next. . . ." Nadar

1854. About *The Meeting*:

> Passant, arrête-toi: c'est Courbet que voici,
> Courbet dont le front pur attend le diadème;
> Et ne t'étonne pas s'il te regarde ainsi:
> Courbet te regardant se regarde lui-même.
>
> Passer-by, stop: Courbet stands here,
> Courbet, whose pure brow awaits a crown;
> And do not be surprised that he regards you thus:
> In looking at you, Courbet is seeing himself.
>
> Gustave Mathieu

1855. About *The Studio:* "I find this rejected picture a masterpiece. I cannot tear myself away from it. . . . But a real man isn't going to be discouraged by a slight setback. . . ." Delacroix's Journal

1860. About *Young Women on the Banks of the Seinè*: "Definitely, Courbet does not understand women . . . ." Champfleury

1865. About Proudhon's portrait:

> Pauvre Proudhon, quel triste sort.
> Depuis trois mois, te voilà mort
> Et Courbet vient te tuer encor....
>
> Poor Proudhon, how sad your fate.
> For three months death has had you,
> And Courbet is going to kill you anew....

1866. About the Salon: "Who would have thought that the great, the unanimous, success of the Salon would be Courbet...." Thoré-Burger

1870. About the Salon: "I do believe that this year will see the defeat of malicious criticism, and unanimous approval of the painter [Courbet]...." Castagnary

1872. "The painter Meissonier recommended that the [Salon] jury declare Courbet not worthy of exhibiting.... the jury ignominiously agreed...." Le Petit Comtois

BIBLIOGRAPHY

COURBET PAPERS. Seven boxes, numbered 1 to 7. Bibliothèque Nationale, cabinet des Estampes.

SILVESTRE, Théophile. *Histoire des Artistes vivants.* Les artistes français, études d'après nature. Paris, Blanchard, 1856.

GROS-KOST, E. *Courbet. Souvenirs intimes.* Paris, Derveaux, 1880.

RIAT, Georges. *Gustave Courbet, peintre.* Paris, Floury, 1906.

CASTAGNARY. *Fragments d'un livre sur Courbet.* Gazette des Beaux-Arts, 1911 (I, II), 1912 (II).

MEIER-GRAEFE, Julius. *Courbet.* Munich, Piper, 1921.

LEGER, Charles, *Courbet.* Paris, Crès, 1929.

LEGER, Charles. *Courbet et son Temps.* Paris, Éditions Universelles, 1948.

COURTHION, Pierre. *Courbet raconté par lui-même et par ses amis.* Geneva, Cailler, I (1948), II (1950).

MAC-ORLAN, Pierre, *Courbet.* Paris, Éditions du Dimanche (Les Demi-Dieux), 1951.

MACK, Gerstle. *Gustave Courbet.* New York, Knopf, 1951.

BULLETIN DES AMIS DE COURBET. Paris, Ornans, 1947-54.